Jelly and Bean can see a dark cloud over the hill. A storm is coming to Follifoot Farm.

Crash! Bang! A clap of thunder sends Jelly and Bean into the barn. Big drops of rain come down in the farmyard.

The rain comes down hard and fast. Water runs off the hill and down to the farm tracks.

The hens and the chickens watch from the hut as the water gets deeper and deeper.

Then the water comes over the top of the pond. A river of water runs to the farmyard.

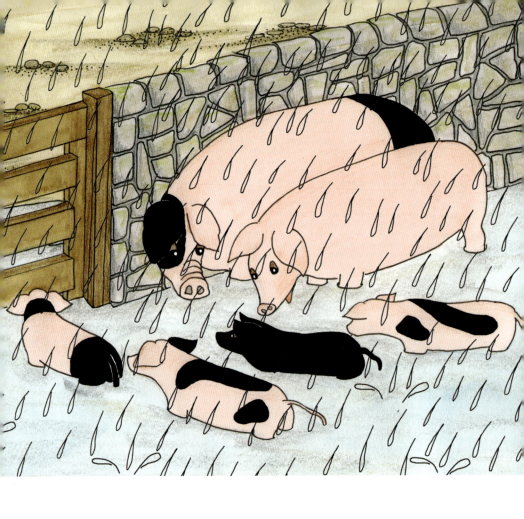

The water rushes into the pigpen. Soon the hut is flooded. The little pigs are afraid.

The farmer comes to let the pigs out of the pen. He sends them into the barn with Jelly and Bean.

They stay in the barn until the rain stops and the water level goes down. They have good fun with Jelly and Bean.